ADULT

Christina Masciotti

BROADWAY PLAY PUBLISHING INC
224 E 62nd St, NY NY 10065
www.broadwayplaypub.com
info@broadwayplaypub.com

ADULT

© Copyright 2017 by Christina Masciotti

All rights reserved. This work is fully protected under the copyright laws of the United States of America. No part of this publication may be photocopied, reproduced, stored in a retrieval system, or transmitted, in any form or by any means, electronic, mechanical, recording, or otherwise, without the prior permission of the publisher. Additional copies of this play are available from the publisher.

Written permission is required for live performance of any sort. This includes readings, cuttings, scenes, and excerpts. For amateur and stock performances, please contact Broadway Play Publishing Inc. For all other rights please contact AO International, Antje Oegel, 917-521-6640, aoegel@aoiagency.com.

Cover photo: Oren R Cohen

First printing: May 2017
I S B N: 978-0-88145-714-8

Book design: Marie Donovan
Typographic controls: Adobe InDesign
Typeface: Palatino
Printed and bound in the U S A

ADULT premiered at Abrons Arts Center on 30 January 2014. The cast and creative contributors were as follows:

STANLEY	Jimmie James
TARA	Betsy Hogg
Director	Ian Morgan
Set	Stephen Dobay
Lights	Driscoll Otto
Sound	Ben Williams
Costumes	Linda Mancini

CHARACTERS & SETTING

STANLEY, *56, a high school dropout and self-employed gun dealer. He still wears battered clothes leftover from his early days as a construction worker.*

TARA, *18, his tech-savvy, girly-girl daughter. Her clothes are form-fitting and bright.*

STANLEY's *row-home in Reading, PA.*

SCENE BREAKDOWN

Scenes 1-4—January
Scenes 5-7—February
Scene 8—May
Scene 9—June
Scene 10—August

Scene 1

(STANLEY's living room features a display of guns for sale on white pegboard panels, a chair that would swallow a smaller man, and a sense of general disrepair. A recently repaired display case hoards more guns for sale. A separate upstairs bedroom is also visible, and a prominent door leads to the street. STANLEY enters holding his cell phone to his ear.)

STANLEY: Yeah, I'm here. You're not allergic to cats. We had a cat for Christsake. No one sneezes like that. You screamed. You felt good, I think my back went out every time. I jumped two feet off the chair. No, I'll tell you what you're doin'. In order to justify your face being swollen, you pretend you're allergic to cats. That's what you say to keep drinking. *(He pulls the phone away from his ear.)* I heard you. Are you done? Look, I just wanted to ask about Tara. Do you know how long she gets off for her winter break? Maybe she could come down, put her feet up for a while. It don't have to be the whole thing, a day, whatever. It's up to her, we can go to the farmer's market, stuff like that. The Amish ladies came out with a new pretzel with chocolate chips. Can you just tell her to call me. Wait, hold on, tell her somethin', would ya? Tell her I said it'd be nice to see her.

(TARA enters eating a chocolate chip soft pretzel. She sits and takes out her cell phone. STANLEY approaches her.)

STANLEY: So how'd your first semester go?

TARA: *(Looking at her phone)* O K.

STANLEY: I guess you were too busy to write. That's O K.

TARA: I called you a few times, but there was no voicemail or anything.

STANLEY: I don't know what's wrong with my phone. Sometimes, you pick it up: seashell.

TARA: That's weird.

STANLEY: I wait all day for Verizon to come. They never show.

TARA: You should stop paying your bill.

STANLEY: Oh, I haven't paid in months. *(Pause)* So what's your major?

TARA: What?

STANLEY: A vet. Isn't that—

TARA: Yeah. I don't know.

STANLEY: Must be a lotta science classes.

TARA: I guess.

STANLEY: Eventually they hit you with all that. How are the tests? Rugged?

TARA: I only had one final. I don't know how I did on it. We're supposed to check through the school's website.

STANLEY: Oh, I have a lap computer, did you see? My buddy, Vic, give it to me to move some business on-line. He's hooked to it, that's how I got you your portable phone, through ebay. It was a trip. *(Pause)* Musta made a lotta new friends up there.

TARA: I didn't really want to.

STANLEY: Why not?

TARA: The people are so narrow-minded. Not only do they all look the same, they all act the same. Jocks that you know, like from the movies. My roommate, Keely, watches T V twenty-four hours a day with her face this close. One time, I said, "I'm studying, could you turn it off, or put in headphones?" She got really pissed off and turned it off. Then she turned on her computer and started playing previews to episodes!

STANLEY: No shit.

TARA: Inside my head, I was stabbing her with Satan's pitchfork.

STANLEY: *(Laughs)* Young and dumb is what I say. *(Pause)* Teachers any good?

TARA: Maybe Ms Kent.

STANLEY: Oh yeah? What's she teach?

TARA: Sociology of Sex, Gender, and Race.

STANLEY: That's a class?

TARA: She was kind of like enthusiastic. But in her own way that's really dull to everyone else. She lets people cheat, so that's cool.

STANLEY: What do you mean?

TARA: For all her exams, everyone turns the brightness down on their phones, and puts them right here. *(Putting her phone on her seat)* It's so obvious. They look up every question.

STANLEY: Were you doin' that?

TARA: I don't have a smartphone.

STANLEY: Town musta been a nice change, though. Your ma said it was by a river.

TARA: There's nothing to do. Sit in your room, and get high. That's what everybody else does. Go to a club and get fucked up from beer or liquor. Or go shopping, nine bucks to the mall, depending on the cab prices, then spend I don't know how much more there. That'll keep me temporarily satisfied. There, like nobody realizes they're unhappy. They're all robots. They suck.

STANLEY: What about studying?

TARA: All the people who studied stayed at the library all day. I don't wanna spend my whole day at the library. I wanna be able to choose what to do.

STANLEY: Is that why you're going to college? To have fun?

TARA: Partly.

STANLEY: To party?

TARA: No, I said partly. Jesus.

STANLEY: O K, O K, I'm just askin'. If I ever went, that would be my top priority. Runnin' the hell around, where's the party, boys? *(Laughs)* You have to live once, right?

TARA: I feel like my life is going around and around in a very small circle, and never advancing at all.

STANLEY: So it's gonna be a little trickier than you thought, that's all. Gotta bend with the blows.

TARA: But I just feel like everything is so lame. I'm living a person I don't wanna be. I'm eighteen. I don't wanna be eighty and be like, I just did what I was supposed to.

STANLEY: Supposed to? You couldn't wait to go up there.

TARA: I know, but I didn't know what it was. I mean college isn't what people think it is. The key to opportunity or whatever. There's so much bullshit going on. Yeah, it's great if you wanna be brainwashed into all this commercialism and money hungry country, stay in school.

STANLEY: What?

TARA: I just don't see what's the point. I don't see my life going anywhere with it. What could I do in ten years? Mediocre job. High rent. Loan payments on top of everything.

STANLEY: Maybe it's not the right school for you. You can switch.

TARA: Yeah, whatever.

STANLEY: You can't just stay there and be miserable. You have things you can do. You don't wanna be a vet anymore. That's O K. Do you know what you wanna be?

TARA: I don't know. I wanna experience my life.

STANLEY: What do you mean you wanna experience your life?

TARA: I don't know. I've always been afraid of change. Right now, I want my life to turn completely upside down. Like even just being back here, I feel like a different person. I feel more of who I really am. *(Pause)* Actually, I was thinking about taking a semester off, and maybe staying here a while.

STANLEY: Here? In Reading?

TARA: Yeah.

STANLEY: Are you shittin' me?

TARA: I don't know how to explain it, but I mean the second I got off the bus, I felt so connected to myself. It's beautiful. You can see the sky. There're trees. It's like so natural, like I don't need to use materialistic things to make me happy. I can see why people spend their whole lives here.

STANLEY: I'll be damned.

TARA: I don't know what I wanna do for my life, and I don't know where I wanna be ten years from now, but right now, I wanna be here. I wanna be in the middle of nowhere.

STANLEY: That's Reading. The middle of nowhere with more crime.

TARA: I'm serious.

STANLEY: I know you are.

TARA: So, what do you think?

STANLEY: Well. I don't have a problem with it. If that's what you wanna do.

TARA: Really?

STANLEY: As a matter of fact, I think it's smart. What you're doin' is: you're thinking for yourself. That takes somethin', not everybody can do that, takes brains to do that. You know you can make whatever you set in mind to do. You make up your mind and you do it. Me too. I didn't ask anyone's approval. I did what I did, and I did it. What later? I might drop dead later. What, what if. You can't live your life what if. If you did, you would never make a move.

TARA: I don't think Mom is gonna go for it.

STANLEY: She don't know?

TARA: Not that I'd be staying with you. I mean I told her I was thinking about taking a semester off, and she lost it. Like anytime I wanna do something that doesn't fit her preferences, she just starts her temper and makes it impossible. Fire and wind come outta her mouth. Whichever way the phone is facing my hair blows back.

STANLEY: Forget her. She don't really know how to be accepting, does she? Looks at you head to toes and corrects everything.

TARA: I know.

STANLEY: I'll tell you something: she's too religious. She's Catholic, and that disturbs her. It don't matter what she thinks. You gotta go your own course. I get it.

TARA: What should I tell her?

STANLEY: Let me handle it. I'll talk to her.

(TARA *exits.* STANLEY *holds his cell phone to his ear. A conversation is in progress.*)

STANLEY: I don't know why you gotta curse on the phone at me. I don't curse at you. You're givin' me a reason right now! I'm not raising my voice, my voice is very low key, O K? You there? No, it was her idea. She come to me. Think about it. All this time, when does she see me? A weekend here, a weekend there. We never got to, you know, it was always short visits. I'm just sayin' that could be a part of it. I'm her old man. Well, I'm still her old man. Alright, don't start that shit with me. You wanna take me through the coals for that now? That's in the past. I'm tryin' to move past the past. *(Pause)* I agree with you, but you just can't tell her that and snap your fingers. It has to seem like her decision. Listen, after a month here she'll be so bored, she'll be dyin' to go back to school. I'll put her to work in the shop, nothin' else sets her straight, that sure as hell will. It'll change her whole look on life.

Scene 2

(TARA *is taking an inventory of guns with* STANLEY.)

STANLEY: Reading's not like you remember, you know? When you were little it was towards the end of being decent. Now it's horrible.

TARA: How is it horrible?

STANLEY: Last month we made the national list that we're the worst city to be.

TARA: The worst?

STANLEY: Top ten.

TARA: What do they base that on?

STANLEY: I don't know how they do it. Maybe they come around and count up the tree-lined blocks that went to a ghetto. A week before you came I was robbed for the second time this year.

TARA: Oh my god. What happened?

STANLEY: A juvenile and two buddies. Second time offender. They caught one, but he won't talk.

TARA: Were you here?

STANLEY: I was sleepin' upstairs and boom. That was some pretty wild shit.

TARA: How'd they get in?

STANLEY: Busted right through. Threw cinder blocks through the front window. Sledgehammers through the displays. Blood all over the place. It was a smash-N-grab. At three A M. Woke me up. Now I roll with a Browning Hi-Power in case I gotta keep myself goin'.

TARA: You should get bars across the window or something.

STANLEY: Yeah, I'm having a gate put in. Fully alarmed.

TARA: When?

STANLEY: Vic does that stuff for me. He's workin' a job in Lancaster this month. Then he might move there. He's leavin' his wife. They had some awful fights. Maybe because they're Italian.

TARA: Well, you can't wait till you get robbed again.

STANLEY: I'll get to it. It ain't like I have so much money, I don't know what to do with it.

TARA: How much did they take?

STANLEY: No way of knowin'. That's why I gotta drop everything, and do a whole store inventory now. Check the numbers against what the book has. The serial number, the model number, the code on the back of the tag. Shit is so boring. Can't do nothin' else, gotta shut down the shop for a week. I told the A T F, I don't have a staff workin' for me, I gotta do all this myself, I have no income for however long it takes me, how am I supposed to get by? Now they raid my ass whenever they goddamn please.

TARA: They do?

STANLEY: Ever since I spoke up.

TARA: What happens when they raid you?

STANLEY: They park their cars backwards, so you can't tell they have government plates, come in 9 to 12 guys in suits, go through all the mumble jumble, askin' to see my logbook, my license, every goddamn record attached to the gun proof of sale. You shoulda seen me the first time it happened. I was so shocked. I wasn't expectin' it. I felt a lotta hot air go into me. I fainted face first on the table. My eyes were open. I don't know who picked me up. (Pause) I was actually ready to sell the place. Fly first class to Octoberfest in Germany and stay there.

TARA: You tried to sell it?

STANLEY: Didn't happen.

TARA: Why not?

STANLEY: All the businesses moved outta Reading a long time ago.

TARA: Why'd they leave? Because of malls and stuff?

STANLEY: Oh hell, yeah. Malls is a part of it. On top
of that, it's the, now we always had ethnic groups.
This area was settled by the Uglo-Saxons. They were
dependable, they adapted. The ones now, they come
with their hands out. Takin' advantage of the country.
Used to be mostly New York. But they're chasin' those
people outta New York like roaches. Like Ehrlich
went up there and sprayed 'em. They're all over now.
There's so many of 'em that we're gettin' to be in the
minority.

TARA: Hallelujah. That's where we belong. The Amish
people, their weird haircuts, and us.

STANLEY: You realize they have a bus on 6th Street,
off Buttonwood, buy the ticket, hop on, it'll take you
right to Mexico. They took over the alley, painting all
colors, blue, yellow, green. Music like you wouldn't
believe. They just discovered stereo boom radios, and
they want everybody within a two block radius to
know they have some really hot Hispanish music, like
caramba, and poor me, a music lover, has to stand by
and listen.

TARA: I was far more offended by all the Stoltzfus
people at the farmer's market. Every stand, their last
name was Stoltzfus. Stoltzfus Bill, Stoltzfus Paul,
Stolzfus John. Plaid shirt, an apron, a smock. Black
bowl Three Stooges cut, freaky beard, no moustache.
They all look like the same nerd.

STANLEY: You don't know what goes on here. Trash
bags open, trash is all over, they throw anything,
they had a sofa sittin' out there, all that filth blockin'
the alley. Soon as the weather warms up they're out
there eating, dyin' their hair, talkin' hours on hours,
nasty noises. Between that and those Puerto Rican
motorbikes. I swear they put a kazoo on the exhaust
pipe.

TARA: It's a different culture, Dad.

STANLEY: It's a very different culture in the alley. Tell me something. Where can we go as a specie with that kind of culture? Nobody has a job to go to. They have tons of families starting from twelve years old. Each one has eight kids followin' 'em.

TARA: Wait, how many kids did Grandma have?

STANLEY: Eleven.

TARA: And twenty-three pregnancies in her lifetime. At least their families stick together. When was the last time you saw your brothers?

STANLEY: All I'm sayin' is, it's no way to live. The men come home drunk, carryin' on. It wakes me up at night. You know those elephants in Africa they shoot anesthesia in a machine gun? I want to shoot 'em to sleep right there from my window. You see that Hummer on Franklin Street? The guy who drives it wears a white stocking on his head. I thought, wow, what a professional guy. They try to come in here. I won't sell to 'em. You should see how much money they flash me, and how pissed they are when they walk outta here empty-handed.

TARA: Dad, you have to be careful.

STANLEY: I'm fine. That's the one perk of growin' up in East New York. I know how to handle myself.

TARA: I don't know. (*Looking at all the guns in the room, she notices* STANLEY's *laptop. She opens it, and turns it on.*)

STANLEY: I just had the place appraised, found out it's worth half what it used to be.

TARA: Why did you have it appraised?

STANLEY: They required it for the loan.

TARA: What loan?

STANLEY: It's a home equity deal.

TARA: What are you getting a loan for?

STANLEY: I'm gonna open up a pistol range in the back. Where the garage used to be. Redo the ground.

TARA: Why?

STANLEY: Reading don't have one. You gotta drive all the way to Mount Penn. The guns they give you are filthy, been dropped a thousand times, shoot 'em, they jam. And they got people, linin' up, waitin' an hour to practice. People are so desperate now. With the N R A crying about the laws might change. Hasn't done shit for me. No one's comin' to Reading to buy a gun.

TARA: They might get shot.

STANLEY: They might get anything. In Kenya, there's a machete massacre every week. You don't hear about that. You hear about the shooting on 10th and Franklin. Well, look who was involved.

TARA: Have you sold anything on-line yet?

STANLEY: Too many glitches.

TARA: Like what?

STANLEY: I'm sitting there spending all my time thinking what buttons to push. Enter. Enter. Enter. Then it's frozen, I'm trying to get it back, it can't be found. It asked me for my mother's maiden name, I got that wrong.

TARA: I can figure that out.

STANLEY: Do you know how to fix my email machine? Glen set it up as "keystonegunstore@enter.net."

TARA: *(Stifling a laugh)* I don't know. That machine might need to be serviced. What's wrong with it?

STANLEY: It's a pain in the ass. I have to spell it for half an hour. And I don't like the word "net." I want simple email. No curly letters. I want "stanley dot com."

TARA: You have to have a curly letter for email. Machines.

STANLEY: O K, then, stanley@home dot com. N'wait. Stanley@period dot com. Not, Stanley, "S." S@S dot com!

TARA: Do you have a website?

STANLEY: How do you do that?

TARA: Just. Where are you selling on-line?

STANLEY: Through, it's called, Gunbroker.com.

TARA: Lemme see.

STANLEY: Why do you tie your shoes at the side?

TARA: Mom made the shoelaces too small. She likes them this way cause she doesn't trip. So she changed mine and made them smaller. She did me a great favor. Look how small the bow is: you can't tie them. What's your log in?

STANLEY: Keystonegun.

TARA: *(Typing)* Password?

STANLEY: Strawberry jam.

TARA: Strawberry jam?

STANLEY: Well, I needed to come up with a password.

TARA: *(Snickers)*

STANLEY: O K, don't embarrass me too bad.

(TARA, *in a fit of giggles, exits.*)

STANLEY: Hey! Don't laugh your guts out!

Scene 3

(A week later. STANLEY *speaks into his cell phone.)*

STANLEY: You know, I can tell already, it's the right thing, her bein' here. This is what she needed to put her on top of her own life. She's lighter, smilier. Listen to this: she had two pictures up on the computer, she goes, "You gotta see the differences". So I get close up to try and see the difference and this scary face jumps out, bleehhhhh! Scared the hell outta me! Yeah, she's a piece of something, but boy, she really threw herself into this computer stuff really hard, she knows it like the back of her palm. She got almost thirty auctions goin' at once. Tell you the truth, I feel sorta rich. Money goes right to my account: Ding. Just shows up. I can barely keep up with the shit I gotta ship out. I think every F F L dealer on the planet is connected to this thing, while I been sittin' on my ass livin' in squander. If anything, I think seein' what she could do for me, got the ball goin' for herself. I think she has a lot of future goals now that she didn't have before. Why? Because of me. Would it kill you to give credit where it deserves for once? That's the best you could do. I'm not the loser you thought I was. I know what a compliment is and compliments don't call people losers. Thanks, you're a sweetheart.

(TARA is in her bed. Feverish, she pulls her cardigan over her head.)

TARA: *(Stuck mid-pull)* Owwwww!

(STANLEY enters with a box of crackers, and a can of Coke.)

STANLEY: What happened to you?

TARA: *(Removing the sweater)* My button got caught.

STANLEY: What?

TARA: My button got caught in my hair. I couldn't move.

STANLEY: Are you O K now?

TARA: Yeah.

STANLEY: Here are your crackers.

TARA: Oh, Dad. I can't eat these.

STANLEY: You picked the box yourself.

TARA: No, you picked the box. You touched it and said, "Do you want these?" I thought they were regular. Peanut butter's too much.

STANLEY: Well, I have plain shoo-fly pie. It's fresh. You like that.

TARA: Mmm. I love eating the contents of a gingerbread man's diaper.

STANLEY: What's your problem?

TARA: Would you wanna eat that if you had a stomach thing?

STANLEY: You have to eat something.

TARA: Do you have any rice?

STANLEY: I have twist pastas. That'll be fun. I'm not used to cookin' big meals. I can fix 'em up my style, with creamed ham and peas.

TARA: Gross. That's so Pennsylvania Dutch.

STANLEY: Well, excuse me all to hell.

TARA: It's O K. I'm not hungry anyway. I know that fucking meal from McDonald's is what got me sick.

STANLEY: McDonald's? Tara, you're a junkeater.

TARA: Who's talkin'?

STANLEY: I'm not the one bringin' bags of chee-cheetos in here. I thought you knew better by now. You should watch what you're eating. You couldn't get me in McDonald's if I was starving and malnourished. Stale food. Sour food. Not even for a drop of something. You're not doin' your body any favor eatin' in there.

TARA: I know. Burger King is so much better.

STANLEY: Right.

TARA: It is. Burger King broils the meat, and it's real meat. And they feed cows beer. They actually serve Angus meat.

STANLEY: A lotta mind blowin' shit goin' on at Burger King.

TARA: McDonald's they like microwave 'em and they're not real meat. I never got sick from Burger King.

STANLEY: Well, have some of your Coke.

(TARA *drinks and grimaces.*)

STANLEY: What's a matter?

TARA: This is so carbonated.

STANLEY: It's supposed to settle your stomach.

TARA: Do you have any Pepsi?

STANLEY: What do you want with Pepsi? You have a Coke right there.

TARA: Pepsi is so less carbonated.

STANLEY: Oh, for crying out loud.

TARA: It's a fact. It's like I'm drinking air, and it doesn't even taste good the air I'm drinking.

STANLEY: I'll run out to Giant and get some Uncle Ben's, but I'm not getting Pepsi. We have Pepsi, it's called Coke. (*He starts to leave.*)

TARA: Wait, Dad.

(STANLEY *stops.*)

TARA: Can you lie to Mom about something?

STANLEY: I'm not lyin' to your ma.

TARA: Why not? You've done it before. You do it all the time.

STANLEY: O K. Maybe that's why I don't wanna do it.

TARA: Oh. I thought it'd be easy for you. Can't you just tell her I'm visiting my friend Vanessa when I go to Stonersville?

STANLEY: Stonersville? What the hell's in Stonersville?

TARA: My boyfriend.

STANLEY: You have a boyfriend?

TARA: Yeah, I do.

STANLEY: I didn't know you had a boyfriend.

TARA: Well, I do.

STANLEY: Since when?

TARA: Last April.

STANLEY: Who? Mikey?

TARA: Mikey?

STANLEY: Didn't he walk you home yesterday?

TARA: Yeah, from the pet store. I don't know why. He has my number memorized and he won't leave me alone. I was bent down touching the puppies and suddenly there he was going: "Guess you're not tired of me." Out of him being pathetic, I'll be like, "Uh-huh." It's like he's seriously an idiot.

STANLEY: Dumb dutchie.

TARA: And he's always trying to give me things, I guess to impress me or whatever. Like he had two Garfield stickers, and he told me I could pick one. I didn't care, I told him to pick the one he liked. He picked Garfield with a teddy bear and hearts, for himself. And gave me Garfield eating a sandwich. I was like, wow, that's not the one I expected you to pick.

STANLEY: So who's this boyfriend?

TARA: His name's LaTuan.

STANLEY: LaTuan? Is he French?

TARA: No.

STANLEY: Where's he from?

TARA: New York. He moved to Stonersville to take care of his aunt.

STANLEY: You know him from school?

TARA: Yeah, he used to hang out near my high school.

STANLEY: Did he go there?

TARA: No, he's not in school.

STANLEY: He's not in school?

TARA: He's dislectic. He had a problem at school. But he has a really high I Q and it shows in his conversation. He's like a full-fledged Democrat, and he's really convincing. In an argument he'll convince you you're wrong, then later admit he knew you were right.

STANLEY: What was he doin' at your high school?

TARA: Hanging out.

STANLEY: How old is he?

TARA: My age.

STANLEY: And he's a dropout?

TARA: He didn't finish school, but he's getting his G E and he's a genius with computers. He taught himself how to do H T M L, and he re-did my Tumblr background in a pink and grey plaid thing with

borders around them. He's so sweet. He got me Adobe
Photoshop free from Bit Lord.

STANLEY: And he asked you to go steady?

TARA: No one says that.

STANLEY: I guess I'm retarded from old age.

TARA: I knew him a long time before we started going
out.

STANLEY: Oh yeah?

TARA: Yeah, a loooong time. We met on March 27th
and we didn't start going out till April 19th. I knew
him, we just weren't going out. I used to see him at his
soccer matches for the Queens World Cup. It's just like
the real World Cup, they start out with sixteen teams,
and they choose a country and get the official jerseys
and everything. He's the captain of Scotland, so he can
fight with the referee and choose their training days.
Then we were on the phone. He was like, "So what do
you wanna do?" I was like, "I don't know, what do you
wanna do?" Cause I didn't think he wanted to have a
relationship, and he didn't think I did, but every time
we saw each other we had that kind of connection.
So he said, "You wanna go out with me, don't you? I
know you wanna go out with me." And he was like,
"Well, I never ask a girl out."

STANLEY: What is he, half-and-half?

TARA: What does half-and-half mean?

STANLEY: Half-gay.

TARA: No. He doesn't ask girls out because he's afraid
of getting hurt. So I said, "Well, I'm not asking you
out." And he goes, "O K, I'm just gonna say it: we're
going out now."

STANLEY: So why can't your ma know?

TARA: Because she wouldn't let me go to the prom with him because he's black.

STANLEY: What?

TARA: She freaked out and made my life miserable. It wasn't enough that she ruined my prom night.

STANLEY: He's black?

TARA: Yeah.

STANLEY: You're dating a black guy? *(Pause)* Tara, a black guy?

TARA: Yeah, what do you want me to say? He's black.

STANLEY: God, Tara.

TARA: What?

STANLEY: I feel woozy.

TARA: Is it your stomach?

(STANLEY *faints.*)

TARA:Dad?

Scene 4

(TARA *speaks into her cell phone.*)

TARA: I didn't watch the game, but I think they won. Because they were jumping on each other's heads with their crotches open. How was your practice? Metamucil is not an energy drink. Unless you feel energized after you take a shit. How can you be so smart and never hear of like a cultural phenomenon for older people? Yeah, I got a bus schedule. You could come here, too, you know, if you wanted. Of course, I told him, my dad doesn't care. At least he's more of my day and age than my mom. Well, in some ways. I don't know. He'd probably take us shooting because he likes to show off the only thing he's good at. It's really fun,

I like the aiming. The first shot is always best because you're surprised about the movement and reflexes are better. Well, I'm sorry. I didn't mean to be insensitive. Forget it, I'd rather meet your aunt, anyway. Yeah, I'm telling you, he'll let me do anything I want. Don't worry about it. Worry about what we're gonna do when I get there.

(STANLEY *stands up at the top of the stairs.*)

STANLEY: Tara! *(He comes downstairs.)*

TARA: You look dishoveled.

STANLEY: Well, do me a favor: next time you're sick, don't get me sick, O K? I been using a lot of Tempos and anti-gas pills, but I still couldn't sleep all night. What saved me was throwing up.

TARA: So have you thought about what I asked you?

STANLEY: Maybe I'm payin' for my sins now, and I won't go to hell when I die.

TARA: Can I go or what?

STANLEY: Unless someone has a voodoo doll of me because in one month I had so many things happen.

TARA: Dad, he's my best friend.

STANLEY: It's too far away.

TARA: I found out there's a bus every hour. I could go and come back in an afternoon.

STANLEY: Buses don't go to Stonersville.

TARA: The one that goes to Philly does.

STANLEY: Well, we're not doing that. I'm gonna nip this in the butt right now: the answer is no, and that's the end.

TARA: What's the big deal? I thought you'd be cool with it.

STANLEY: I talked to your mother about it.

TARA: What! What did you say?

STANLEY: I told her you wanted to see him.

TARA: Why did you have to call her!

STANLEY: I'm not sorry that I did, Tara. She told me more than I had to say.

TARA: What did she tell you?

STANLEY: She said he smoked himself stupid.

TARA: Oh my god! He doesn't smoke.

STANLEY: No? He's not involved with drugs?

TARA: She thinks he is!

STANLEY: Tara, don't fuck with me. I'll bat ya out.

TARA: He's not anymore.

STANLEY: Well, good, I'm glad.

TARA: He doesn't sell drugs. He did a long time ago, but he didn't want to get too into the game. He stopped.

STANLEY: Why do you think he was hanging out by your high school that he didn't go to?

TARA: He was friends with my friends.

STANLEY: Your friends who get kicked out of every camp for weed?

TARA: It's not what you think, O K? He's a complicated guy.

STANLEY: Tara, when you walk like a duck, you look like a duck.

TARA: He's a great guy.

STANLEY: That ain't what you wanna get caught up in. It has trouble written on it.

TARA: Dad—

STANLEY: You know, you kicked up a big fuss, I thought maybe you wanted to come back and start from all over again. But this is makin' more sense now. I figured it out. It took a while.

TARA: What did you figure out?

STANLEY: This is why you're back here. This kid. Not cause of the goddamn trees in Reading. And sure as hell not cause of me.

TARA: No, Dad—

STANLEY: You lied to me. You know I can put up with a lot of things. One thing I can't stand the most are liars. I'm not lying to your mother. You wanna see him, you have to tell her.

TARA: Did you tell her that he moved to Pennsylvania?

STANLEY: No.

TARA: Can you at least not tell her anything else about it? She thinks I broke up with him.

STANLEY: How long are you planning to keep this from her?

TARA: I can't say anything other than what a fucking flying nun you are! So honest and forthright all of a sudden. *(She go upstairs.)*

Scene 5

(A few weeks later. STANLEY *speaks into his cell phone, holding a bottle of laundry detergent.)*

STANLEY: Let me ask you somethin'. I bought some Ajax. It's not gonna bleach her clothes, is it? *(Reading the label)* It doesn't say bleach or bleaching action, but it's a white bottle. I'm not paranoid, I just remember the fit she threw when you ruined her jeans, and I have enough fits to deal with right now. *(Pause)* Yeah, well, talkin' to her is easier said than done. She just shuts me up by outbursting. It's different for you. I was already on a thin line. She wants me to sit back and say I don't give a fuck, like I did her whole childbirth. That's all she thought I was good for. I mean I never expected to get off scotch free, but I thought I could do somethin'. Sheesh. I sound like a whiner. I'm not in a good state of mind right now. *(Pause)* That's exactly what we're focusin' on is school, that's right. She's ready, yeah, she got the catalogs goin', the applications, this deadline, that one, she's all over that shit.

(STANLEY hangs up and enters TARA's room. She has earbuds in.)

STANLEY: Hey, what are you listenin' to?

TARA: Music.

STANLEY: Where is it coming from?

(TARA flashes her tiny MP3.)

STANLEY: Oh, look at that. That's pretty neat.

TARA: What judgment were you gonna make?

STANLEY: *(Louder)* I said, that's pretty neat.

TARA: Who are you to say that!

STANLEY: Take that stuff outta your ears for a second.

TARA: Why?

STANLEY: Because we're havin' a fuckin' conversation.

(TARA takes out her earbuds. STANLEY is unsure how to proceed.)

STANLEY: Was there a newspaper this morning?

TARA: Yeah, I left it on the table.

STANLEY: Was there a Garfield cartoon?

TARA: I have no idea.

STANLEY: Did you see the one I cut out for you?

TARA: No.

STANLEY: Oh. You gotta read it. Garfield's in court. They call a witness: "Meegenralsodonorishasissimo." And the judge goes, "Please state your name. And spell your last name." *(Laughs)* Ah, that's a classic. *(Pause)* So. Have you heard from Berks Campus?

TARA: No.

STANLEY: Did you turn in your application on time?

TARA: I told you the deadline already passed when I decided to apply.

STANLEY: Tara, the edge to your voice.

TARA: I can edge my voice whenever I want. It's my voice.

STANLEY: Well, so what happens now?

TARA: I don't know what happens now.

STANLEY: You can't live your life like that. You need to strategy plan, A, B, C.

TARA: So I applied to Berks Campus. If they have a spot, they'll let me in, if not, I have to wait till the next cycle.

STANLEY: Then what are you gonna do till then?

TARA: What do you care? You were fine with it until Mom changed your mind.

STANLEY: Your mother didn't change my mind.

TARA: Then why are you being such an asshole?

STANLEY: Don't gimme lip like that. That never went when I was young. I woulda been eatin' concrete, pickin' my teeth up off the ground.

(TARA rolls her eyes.)

STANLEY: You have a real crummy attitude, you know that? You're 18. You got years to screw up your life, you don't gotta do that now.

TARA: I'm not, you are. Every chance you get.

STANLEY: Oh, that's good.

TARA: I didn't tell you about LaTuan, so you and Mom would start ganging against me. I confided in you and you betrayed me!

STANLEY: All I told her is you were askin' to see him.

TARA: That was enough for her to lose trust in me. Now every time we talk she has a million questions.

STANLEY: O K, well at some point, no matter how hard you try to keep it, she's gonna find out anyways.

TARA: At some point, but not at the worst possible time when she totally controls my life. Did it ever occur to you what she would do if she found out he was living here?

STANLEY: I was thinkin' about you, Tara, not her.

TARA: Were you thinking it would be the end of everything for me? Because it would be! She'd probably send me outta state or something.

STANLEY: Iowa State?

TARA: Maybe Iowa, who knows.

STANLEY: Tara, that leads to be seen.

TARA: Oh my god, you have no idea. She'll do whatever it takes to keep me away from him.

STANLEY: Shit, I was just tryin' to look out for ya.

TARA: I don't need anyone to stand over me.

STANLEY: Tara you ain't in school, and you got no plans to go back—

TARA: Not everybody has school in the background. Look at Bill Gates.

STANLEY: Look at me. You're talkin' about 500 fortune people. So happened Bill Gates was involved in a business that was a world necessity. He was up to date with electronics. College wouldn't offer him anything. The whatever college offers. But you're still findin' the profession you wanna keep busy with. You need to get exposed to things, to learn the rules that the society goes by, to get more ideas on how to deal with people. You know, you're wasting a lotta time here. You have to be reasonable.

TARA: That goes both ways.

STANLEY: Come off it. You know you need to concentrate on whatever it is, gettin' a credit somewhere.

TARA: I won't be able to concentrate on anything until I see my boyfriend!

STANLEY: Don't go into a little tizzy.

TARA: Why can't I see him? I have things to give him that he needs. T-shirts. C Ds, clothes. He needs his stuff. I can't send him packages, they get stolen.

STANLEY: Can you stop panicking for a second? He's not gonna die without his stuff.

TARA: I told him I would give it to him! He's my boyfriend. I haven't seen him since he moved here. And it's our anniversary. We always spend it together every month, we made a pact with each other, and I already missed two! Can you understand how I feel?

STANLEY: You have an anniversary every month?

TARA: On the 19th.

STANLEY: Of every month?

TARA: We celebrate it.

STANLEY: That's not an anniversary.

TARA: We made plans and I told him I was coming! I can't back out. If I don't see him in person soon he'll never speak to me again.

STANLEY: Uh-oh, doomsday.

TARA: He has untreatable depression, he can't help it. He gets upset and he withdraws from the world.

STANLEY: Tara, I don't mean to pop your balloon, but the guy's a fuckin' mess.

TARA: You have no idea what he's been through. He's been on his own since he was twelve. He used to be beaten when he was young. And his mother's boyfriend shot and killed his four year old brother when he was five years old.

STANLEY: Why the fuck would you wanna be involved with someone like that?

TARA: You don't understand. Everybody lets him down all the time, everyone he has grown to love has either died right in front of him, was murdered, or died of old age. I'm not gonna abandon him! There's no reason why I can't see him. It's not like it's some vacation or something. It's the right thing to do! His aunt is in the hospital with Chrome's disease and a staple through her stomach. He needs my support.

STANLEY: Why don't he come to you, then?

TARA: He can't.

STANLEY: You shouldn't be goin' after anybody. If he wanted to see you, he would come to you. Tara, he's playin' you. Listen, I'm not sayin' this to upset you, but those are the kind of people who use people. What you're gonna learn eventually is that it's not worth it, getting involved with someone like that because you don't wanna deal with his problems.

TARA: Dad, he's a good person, thoughtful, sensitive, caring—

STANLEY: You left one word outta that sentence: ZERO. He's zero. It pulls you down that kind of person. Their problems hindrance your development. You won't be treated well by someone like that because they don't know how to do it. It takes so much energy from you. It feels the same over and over. It's overwhelming.

TARA: Well, that's what it means, the love of your life—

STANLEY: Whoa, whoa, whoa, stop the bullshit.

TARA: —that's complete love, ups and downs—

STANLEY: If he had a basement full of bodies in the freezer you could come up with some kinda William Shakespeare shit.

TARA: You're jumping to all kinds of things when you haven't even met him!

STANLEY: I don't have to meet him, I don't have to know him—

TARA: You know he's black and that's all you need to know.

STANLEY: No, hey, Tara, you're missing the picture. I'm not a racist.

TARA: Whatever.

STANLEY: I don't believe one race is better. People are people. There's not that much difference across people. And I can tell you something happens to people when they start dealing drugs.

TARA: Here we go.

STANLEY: It doesn't matter he stopped, it matters that he started in the first place.

TARA: You're harping on this drug thing and it has nothing to do with anything.

STANLEY: Yes it does, you know why? Because doing drug dealing you learn to take chances and that becomes a lifestyle. People who do that kind of thing look at women as accessories rather than equal human things. Like who's the other pimp who likes to dress in white?

TARA: Now he's a pimp?

STANLEY: Pay attention to what I'm saying! You grab one word and take off. I didn't say he was a pimp. I'm saying one form or another they learn to do the same thing. It's like they have no conscious. You don't wanna be involved with that, socializing with the gutter. We're looking for preppy kind of people. You went to a prep school among all those people who travel all over the world. So worldly. It's a great big open world to you.

TARA: Exactly! I need to learn from my own experiences!

(TARA *goes downstairs.* STANLEY *follows.*)

STANLEY: Not to mention who the hell gave you the right to mix our blood? It's not just black. It's black, Chinese. If you brought a chung chung here I would say the same thing.

TARA: What are you talking about!

STANLEY: You're tellin' me how serious it is. That's the next step of serious. You wanna take your kid to the park and have people yell, "Chung chung lover", or "Nigger lover", or "Spic lover". *(Pause)* Don't shake your head. Tara, I'm tellin' you straight. I don't fool around the bush. If I can't speak honestly with you, then what's the point?

TARA: There is no point. Stop talking.

STANLEY: Have you thought about the customs?

TARA: Like you know anything about it.

STANLEY: Have you ever had black food? It's all fried. Sweet, greasy shit, you don't know what it is—

TARA: It's better than scrapple!

STANLEY: Tara, let me finish my thought, O K? In the black community it's normal to beat your wife—

TARA: If you're trying to scare me, it's working. I've never been more afraid of you in my entire life!

STANLEY: Puerto Ricans drown the kids of their ex-husbands—

TARA: Oh fuckin' god.

STANLEY: It's the truth, Tara, they have this sense of honor, don't turn your nose, read some history, read the paper.

TARA: You know what was in the papers about Irish people in the 1800s? Pictures of drunk apes sitting on barrels of rum!

STANLEY: Listen, how will you understand what I'm trying to say if you keep cutting me off?

TARA: It's a propogandic tactic so people can look down on each other like you look down on the alley. It's all like tools of oppression, and you don't even see it because you were too stupid to even graduate ninth grade!

STANLEY: Hey! I know you go through these moods where you think you're all-knowing, but you might learn something if you could actually shut the hell up and listen. Ain't what you wanna hear? Too bad! You know how many things I wish I never heard? I'm fifty-six years old, I deserve to hear things that make some fuckin' sense! *(Grabbing her shoulders)* STRAIGHTEN YOUR ASS UP! *(Releasing her and calming down)* This is how people communicate and exchange information, Tara.

TARA: Can't you go out of your way for me for once in your life?

STANLEY: What do you think I'm doin' here?

TARA: You didn't pay for my high school. You didn't even come to my graduation.

STANLEY: Your graduation? Your mother didn't want me there.

TARA: It's never your fault.

STANLEY: Your mother and I were at odds. That's how at odds we were.

TARA: Keep your problems with my mom to yourself.

STANLEY: But that was all your mother's fault. The cause and effect was her.

TARA: See what I mean?

STANLEY: Tara, I can't come to everything. Your ma and I can't always make it to everything.

TARA: Don't make you and my mom the same thing! She always does! YOU NEVER DO! THAT'S A HUGE DIFFERENCE!

STANLEY: O K. You just got very excited there. I'm glad you're expressing how you feel.

TARA: You never reached out to me. You sent birthday gifts through snail mail so they came a week late. You think that counts for anything? It's more personal communication like using Skype or FaceTime that makes a difference.

STANLEY: Tara, I don't even know what you're talking about.

TARA: How dare you stop paying child support when I turned eighteen. You washed your hands about me.

STANLEY: Tara, my job—

TARA: It's not your job, it's your mentality!

STANLEY: Your mother tell you that?

TARA: All you do is pay my phone bill! You buy me a phone for my birthday, something from the dinosaur time, you didn't even pay 20 dollars for it. I looked it up on ebay and the bidding started at 99 cents!

STANLEY: I had to tighten up expenses around your birthday.

TARA: Because you have dry spells forever!

STANLEY: I don't got much power over that, do I?

TARA: After a year of dry spell you look for extra work. It doesn't work that way, the bills keep coming in. You have to find work. You're not the only one with financial problems!

STANLEY: I didn't say I was, did I?

TARA: You took money under the table not to pay child support! We had to petition the court. Checks came. Eleven dollars. Twenty-four dollars. I don't know why mom endorsed them, fold and tear, fold and tear, fifteen dollars! Wow! Thanks, Dad!

STANLEY: Look, don't hold my life record against me now, I'm tryin'—

TARA: Mom was starting a business on her own. One person worked for her who she couldn't pay. We had to move to pay for my first semester of college. We had to move to a smaller place. You didn't pay for my education. One thing I need your help with, and you can't do it!

STANLEY: O K, your body has all that adrenaline rush and you need to calm yourself.

(TARA *puts on an enormous puff coat.*)

TARA: I didn't know how lucky I was to be spared any fucking connection to you.

STANLEY: Where you goin'?

TARA: I'm eighteen years old! Hello, you know what freedom is? It's a right. I can do whatever I want.

(TARA *grabs a bag, and exits through the front door.*)

Scene 6

(STANLEY *speaks into his cell phone.*)

STANLEY: Yeah, have you heard from Tara? Nothing, I thought maybe she called you. She's not gone. I just don't know where she, uh, is right now. Well, I don't have her in a cage here. Are you gonna go braserk, now? Don't call the police. A few hours. What are you worried about? Stop it, nothin' happened. Tara wouldn't do nothin' like that. Because she's like a flower. She's a hippie. She's a good kid. (*Lying*) Sure, her stuff's here. Actually, oh wait, here she left me a note. Look at that. It says, "I went to, uh. Burger King. I'll be right back." (*Fake laugh*) I know this is nothing to laugh at, but it is a joke, ain't? Here she got us all worked up, and she only took a cab over to Burger King. (*Fake laugh*) Yeah, my car is outta order on accounta. In-air-sha. How do you say it? What happens is, you step on the gas and it pops backwards like. Yeah, it just stalls. O K, so. You good? I don't want you sufferin' like a basket case all night. Tara is fine. You can relax, I'll have her call ya.

(STANLEY *hangs up. Two hours later. He paces in* TARA's *room. He opens his phone, pushes a button, and puts the phone to his ear.*)

STANLEY: Tara. This is your father. No need to say, I am upset. Where are you? This is not how you handle

your problems, either the way you want it, or take
the highway. Call me when you get this. *(He hangs up.
Another hour passes. He paces in his living room and calls
her again.)* Turn your goddman phone on! My blood is
boiling, you know that? How long you know this kid,
not even a whole year, and you treat him better than
your own father? I'll tell you what, if I don't hear back
from you in the next thirty minutes, I'm calling your
mother, and I'm telling her everything, so you better
get on the horn pronto.

(Later that night. STANLEY *can barely stay awake in his
chair. He speaks into his phone.)*

STANLEY: Oh, boy. This turned into a huge thing. You
know, you gotta realize things seem worse at night.
Things that happen at night seem dark and heavy. In
the morning, it's nothing. Give it some time to breathe.
I didn't call your ma, O K? This is just between us. I
won't tell her nothin'. I know I musta upset ya pretty
bad. I'm not a people's person, O K? I just want you to
know, I'm here. I'm not goin' anywhere till I hear from
you. Let me know you're O K.

Scene 7

(The only light is an eerie glow from the gun display case.
STANLEY *is asleep on his chair with his phone on his chest.
The door rattles.)*

STANLEY: *(Opening his eyes; disoriented)* Hey.

(The door rattles again.)

STANLEY: Who's there? Hello?

*(*STANLEY *gets up. The door rattles again.)*

STANLEY: Hey! You hear me? Tara?

(No answer. The door rattles again. STANLEY *takes out his
gun and aims it at the door.)*

STANLEY: *(Cocking the hammer)* You fuckers! You think you're comin' back for seconds? Get the fuck off my porch!

(STANLEY puts his finger on the trigger.)

TARA: Dad!

STANLEY: *(Accidentally squeezing the trigger and firing the gun)* Tara?

(TARA screams.)

STANLEY: *(Putting the gun down)* TARA! *(He scrambles for his keys to the deadbolt.)* Hold on, Tara, I'm coming. Hold on. *(The lock is stuck.)* C'mon, open, open, open, open!

(The door bursts open. TARA is hunched over in her enormous puff coat, crying.)

STANLEY: Oh god, Tara.

(STANLEY picks TARA up, and brings her inside. Full lights come on.)

STANLEY: *(Frantically trying to examine her)* Here, lemme see. Oh, Jesus, are you O K?

(STANLEY puts TARA's down, and crouches over her, opening her coat.)

TARA: What are you doing?

STANLEY: Honey, I have to get your coat off, lemme see. How bad is it? God help me.

TARA: *(Wriggling away)* Dad, you didn't. I'm O K. I was just scared.

(STANLEY drops his head.)

TARA: I should've rang the doorbell. I didn't wanna wake you.

(STANLEY is in tears.)

TARA: Dad, you know I'm fine, right?

STANLEY: *(Composing himself)* Talk about fuckin' something up. *(Pause)* Boy, I really perspired myself. Do me a favor. Get me a baby aspirin.

(TARA exits and returns with a pink aspirin and a glass of water. STANLEY drinks.)

TARA: Sorry, I couldn't call you. I was just too upset.

STANLEY: Have a nice time then?

(TARA shrugs.)

STANLEY: Give him his stuff back?

TARA: Yeah.

STANLEY: You didn't do nothin' special? For your anniversary and all?

TARA: Sort of. We went to a bay.

STANLEY: A bay?

TARA: It's like a beach, but nobody swims in it cause it's a bay. We were skipping stones. Then we went to White Castle and got ten hamburgers and two mixed milkshakes.

STANLEY: Right, right. Good for you.

Scene 8

(Three months later. STANLEY is catatonic on his chair. TARA enters.)

TARA: We need to talk. *(Pause)* I got into Kutztown.

STANLEY: Oh yeah? Jeez, Tara. That ain't how you start off good news. We-need-to-talk's for when you're about to cry the blues. That's terrific. I didn't even know you applied there.

TARA: They're the strongest with the program I wanna go into.

STANLEY: Computers?

TARA: No, accounting.

STANLEY: Accounting?

TARA: Yeah, I always liked math and numbers, and organizing.

STANLEY: Man, I hate math. You ever see the exclamation point they put on numbers? I used to be so fuckin' confused by that. THREE! *(Pause)* So, that's what it's gonna be then, Kutztown?

TARA: Yeah.

STANLEY: That won't be too bad a commute from here.

TARA: Oh. Dad, I'm not commuting.

STANLEY: What?

TARA: I'm gonna live on campus.

STANLEY: How come?

TARA: Well, it's really cool around there. When I visit LaTuan that's where we end up cause Stonersville doesn't have anywhere good to eat.

STANLEY: Speaking of Latuan, you hear what happened at Wawa?

TARA: No.

STANLEY: An idiot walked in, sprayed the cashier with gasoline, and put him on fire. His shoes melted onto his feet. Cause someone looked at his girlfriend. That's the whole thing. That's how they respond. That's how they communicate. I'm sure the girlfriend is very happy the boyfriend did something to protect her.

TARA: What does that have to do with LaTuan?

STANLEY: Nothing. I just thought about it. *(Pause)* So where would you be livin'?

TARA: In a dorm.

STANLEY: What if they stick you with a room partner like you had before?

TARA: They have a lottery for singles.

STANLEY: That sounds like a gamble.

TARA: Dad—

STANLEY: I'm just sayin' look at what you have here. Could be the best of both worlds. Go there, have your studies, then come back here, no distractions.

TARA: Like my boyfriend.

STANLEY: I didn't say that.

TARA: You think I'm basing my whole decision on him.

STANLEY: The point is, a good school like that has you workin' from dawn up to dawn down. You might appreciate havin' your own room where it's peaceful and quiet, you can concentrate on what's important.

TARA: There's plenty of peace and quiet on campus, and this is what you wanted, by the way, me back at school.

STANLEY: I wanted you back at school, but not like this.

TARA: Like what?

STANLEY: So quick.

TARA: I'm not leaving till August.

STANLEY: August! School don't start in September no more?

TARA: Orientation for transfers starts August 21st.

STANLEY: What's the rush? Jesus, you just got here.

TARA: I've been here since January!

STANLEY: Shit, Tara. That don't give us much time.

TARA: For what?

STANLEY: For anything. Fix up your room for starters.

TARA: My room?

STANLEY: You said you wanted to sponge paint it maroon.

TARA: Well, five months later, I gave up on that.

STANLEY: I got the stuff for you in the basement. I just never got around to it. I thought we could take up the rug, too, and refurnish the floor, sand it down—

TARA: We can still do all that. We have a couple months.

STANLEY: What would be the point if you're not even gonna be around?

TARA: Fine, forget it.

STANLEY: What about the auctions?

TARA: Everything's set up. You just have to keep it going.

STANLEY: I can't manage that by myself.

TARA: It's super easy. You just have to click on a link—

STANLEY: It's too annoying. Don't forget, I'm putting that pistol range out back. That'll get this money thing poppin'.

(TARA *is doubtful.*)

STANLEY: Think about it: an indoor range is far and few. In the cold: it's heated. It'll give me a core customer base. I could even probably work something out with the Reading police officers taking training. We're talking about a range fee of twenty bucks. Five bucks to rent the earmuffs, three for the gloves. The ammunition. Where's my computer? (*He finds a klunky calculator*) That's my computer. That's how complicated it is, and it has big things to press in case you don't see. So if ten people come through, that'd be five hundred bucks. In one day. That's a good gig.

A steady gig. Watch and see. In the long run, it's just what I need to bounce back.

TARA: Right. In Lululand.

STANLEY: Huh?

TARA: You talk with a pride about something that has nothing to do with reality. Reality is, you need money. I found a way to keep you going with times and bring good money in, and you're just gonna scrap that.

STANLEY: You're the one who's leavin' it go.

TARA: I set it up for you. And I went to a lot of trouble and obviously I shouldn't have bothered.

STANLEY: No, you shouldn't have cause it was a lousy idea.

TARA: Thanks.

STANLEY: Somebody who's past their prime time don't mix with computers.

TARA: You won't sit down for five minutes and go through the steps with me.

STANLEY: I never said I would.

TARA: I don't know what you think is gonna happen if you actually try something new. You might find out you're not as useless as you think you are. You act like you have some infliction keeping you in that chair for months on end. You don't have to lift a finger, I'm busy working around the clock to keep your budget out of jeopardy. You just keep ignoring everything in that stupid, sick world of yours. What a life.

STANLEY: I'm sorry I'm such a disappointment to you, but the feeling is mutual.

(TARA *starts to go upstairs.*)

STANLEY: *(Pause)* That come out wrong. Tara. Wait.

(TARA *stops.*)

STANLEY: I didn't mean that. I just. There's a lot I wanted to do while you were here, and now you're leavin. I gotta say, you know, you're gonna be missed.

TARA: It's not like you'll never see me again.

STANLEY: At least we're on the same wave level about one thing: you're better off without me, always were.

TARA: That's not—

STANLEY: Useless like you said. No wonder you're hittin' the pike.

TARA: I just wanna be on my own, that's all.

STANLEY: Course you do. I almost fuckin' killed you for Christsake. I hope you can accept my forgiveness someday.

TARA: Dad, it was an accident, there's nothing to forgive. Plus, it's one more thing I get to never tell mom which beats out painting my nails as my new favorite hobby.

STANLEY: Why tell her? So she can go off the deep edge? She already knows I'm a worthless piece of shit, she doesn't need anymore proof. You're the only thing that's good in my life cause I had nothin' to do with you. I'm sorry, Tara. You come to me with good news, only thing I should be sayin' is, "Congratulations". Congratulations, Tara, congratulations.

TARA: O K, you don't have to keep saying it.

STANLEY: What else can I say? I'd like to make a toast.

TARA: What?

STANLEY: I don't have a drink, but anyways. (*Raising his empty hand up to her*) To Tara. You're goin' to Kutztown. Good goin'. I mean it.

Scene 9

(A month later. STANLEY *enters as* TARA *comes downstairs.)*

TARA: So much for Kutztown!

STANLEY: What's all this now?

TARA: She knows!

STANLEY: What, your ma? What's she know?

TARA: About LaTuan!

STANLEY: How? I didn't tell her.

TARA: She called my cell, and LaTuan picked up like a dumbass. God, why did he have to pick up!

STANLEY: So was it like a heated argument or a fight argument?

TARA: She made me spit the guts of everything!

STANLEY: O K. So you're on her crap list for a while, big whoop.

TARA: Now she won't pay my tuition unless I break up with him!

STANLEY: Oh.

TARA: I'm gonna call her back and tell her off.

STANLEY: Hold on. She's waiting for you to call her back so there can be more argument and that won't change nothin'. God forbid, she be a little bit mellow about somethin'.

TARA: She's such a bitch!

STANLEY: Look, you know, you need to see this for what it is, Tara. This, your ma, you can't listen to her. When she talks, I do the opposite thing automatically.

TARA: She thinks I have low self-esteem.

STANLEY: Well, hers is a little too high. She's hallusional.

TARA: She doesn't even know what her problems are! She doesn't wanna face her problems.

STANLEY: Yeah, ditto.

(TARA *starts crying.*)

STANLEY: Oh boy.

TARA: *(Crying)* All I did was tell her the truth.

STANLEY: I know. I know that. All you're doin' is who you are. You are who you're bein'. You're the independent type like me. I mean, it's in your gene. I never followed the Jones's. We're two fuckin' lemons from the same fuckin' tree, you and me.

TARA: *(Crying)* She said. She said. Um.

STANLEY: What?

TARA: *(Crying)* All the love she had for me was hanging by a thread.

STANLEY: Oh, she don't mean that.

TARA: She meant it. She said. Um. If I decide to continue the relationship.

STANLEY: What?

TARA: *(Crying)* She wants me to forget about her, forget she's my mother. That's how she wants it.

STANLEY: No, she don't. She'll get over it.

TARA: She thinks she can actually blackmail me and I'll do whatever she says!

STANLEY: Tara, when you're your own adult you can do whatever you want. Right now—

TARA: My life doesn't have to abye by her! I'm not a toddler.

STANLEY: O K.

TARA: I have a lot of experience with life. I worked
for two companies. I held a serious, long-distance
relationship for almost nine months. I pay for
everything but food and living places, and school, and
my phone. Maybe I'm not a fully developed adult, but
I'm a good portion of my way there, and I can get the
rest of the way myself!

STANLEY: Hold on—

TARA: I could never go to her anyway. If I had a
problem, I couldn't turn to either of you cause I'm
always rejected.

STANLEY: Hey—

TARA: At least now, I won't keep on hurting myself
because I won't expect anything from either of you.
LaTuan says it's better that way, he's right.

STANLEY: Look, O K, I know your ma. I'm not downing
nobody, but she can't even get along with her clothing
that she's wearing, let alone people. There's no way
around that. How the fuck you think I ended up in
Reading? You cut people off thinkin' that'll make it
better, that makes it worse. I tell ya. It's amazing how
miserable a person can be. Don't cut yourself off. You
don't have to. Not from me.

TARA: It doesn't matter. It's over.

STANLEY: What's over?

TARA: The financial aid deadline already passed.
There's nothing I can do.

STANLEY: What do you mean? You're not goin'?

TARA: I have no choice.

STANLEY: Tara, how many transfer applications did
they have, and they picked you? A lot more than they
let in, I know that much. That's how they do it. They

don't just let anybody in. They want you. If you don't go now, that'll always be the creeps you can't reach.

TARA: What?

STANLEY: Crepes. Don't you know the fairytale story? You have to go. Mush right on, work hard, get the initials behind your name. You're very close to that, you can't stop now. I have it counted down, three more years, then you got the world in your hand.

TARA: I'm not breaking up with him.

STANLEY: It don't have to come to that. We'll work somethin' out. I can help you.

TARA: The tuition is due June 10th. You can't do anything about that.

STANLEY: Your tuition'll be paid.

TARA: How?

STANLEY: Don't worry about it.

TARA: Are you gonna talk to mom about it?

STANLEY: Yeah, that's what I'm gonna do. I'm gonna talk to your mother. Please.

TARA: Well, you don't have the money.

STANLEY: I don't? Last time I checked, I was rollin' in it.

TARA: But that's your loan money.

STANLEY: So?

TARA: That's for your shooting range.

STANLEY: Not no more.

TARA: You had a plan and everything all worked out.

STANLEY: Now I got a better one.

TARA What, to throw away your whole future?

STANLEY: (Laughs) I don't have a future. I'm at the end of my future. Only future I got is you.

Scene 10

(Two months later. STANLEY calls out to TARA.)

STANLEY: Hey, Tara, the phone's workin'.

(TARA enters with a piece of luggage.)

STANLEY: It's workin'.

TARA: Good.

STANLEY: You can call me on my wireless or this one. Whatever's easier.

TARA: O K.

STANLEY: You got both numbers?

TARA: I think so.

STANLEY: Wanna check?

TARA: I'm kind of in the middle of something. *(She opens her luggage and organizes a few things.)*

STANLEY: Do me a favor, call me on this one first. If I don't answer, call my wireless. If I don't answer that, what you do is, leave a message.

TARA: I know how to make a phone call, Dad.

(STANLEY sits down in front of his laptop.)

STANLEY: Come sit over here. I don't know what I'm doing.

TARA: You have to learn to do it by yourself. Follow my directions.

(TARA closes her luggage, and goes to her room. STANLEY reads from a notebook.)

STANLEY: "Plug it in. The light is on the push button below the light. Button has a circle with a line on it. Wait until screen changes. Enter password: BIG DUTCH." Very funny. O K, I plugged it in and the light is on. Now it says: "USE NAME STANLEY

BURNS." STANLEY BURNS is on a white label. Then it says: "password," and there's a white line. I'm supposed to put the password there?

TARA: *(From her room)* Yep. Type it in.

STANLEY: Let me put, BIG DUTCH. It didn't write it. It has 3 X's.

TARA: *(From her room)* That's so no one can read it.

STANLEY: *(Reading)* "Move the arrow with finger in a sliding motion." No kidding. Where's the arrow? Oh! There's the arrow. Oh! I did it! You have to be very gentle, it jumps, don't it? O K, I'm going closer. Very gentle to the password. Now it has one line. *(Reading)* "Click the left button." Let's put BIG DUTCH in there. It keeps on doing crosses like the embroidery Grandma does. As many letters as I do, it keeps putting crosses. There's a line that's following it forward. *(To* TARA*)* This is a disaster.

TARA: *(From her room)* It's fine. That's the cursor. I told you the crosses are so no one can read it. Just type it and hit enter.

STANLEY: At least I can plug it in.

TARA: *(From her room)* You're doing good, just keep going.

STANLEY: *(Reading)* "Caps lock, Delete, Shift, Enter. The curve has to be in front."

TARA: *(From her room)* The cursor. Moving it to the right can go from different folders.

STANLEY: The cursor is the round circle of the line on top?

TARA: *(From her room)* What?

STANLEY: The cursor is on my left and it cannot move.

TARA: *(From her room)* That's not it.

STANLEY: I'm getting it. I'm getting how to move the arrow. *(Reading)* "Wait for the hourglass to disappear." What did you tell me to do? Tara? Taaaara!

TARA: *(From her room)* What!

STANLEY: What's my email computer word?

TARA: *(From her room)* You have to log in before you can do that.

STANLEY: What? *(Reading)* "Enter equals changes the line. Shift equals one capital. Delete equals Backspace."

(TARA enters the living room.)

TARA: *(Dropping an armful of things into her luggage)* Delete erases it.

STANLEY: Oh, I learned that, thank god. Maybe I should click Delete. *(Scanning keys)* A lotta arrows here. How do you know what Delete is? Does it say Delete?

TARA: It's a button.

STANLEY: No shit.

(TARA returns to her room. STANLEY gets up suddenly and his knee goes out.)

STANLEY: Awh!

(STANLEY crumbles to the floor. TARA enters the living room.)

TARA: What happened?

STANLEY: My knee's out. *(Massaging it)* Hurts like a motherfucker.

TARA: What did you do?

STANLEY: I just got up.

TARA: Is it gonna be O K?

STANLEY: Yeah, it's nothin'. It got twisted. *(Barely able to stand)* That's better. *(Limping absurdly)* Just takes a sec.

TARA: Here.

(TARA *helps* STANLEY *back to his chair, and returns to her room.*)

STANLEY: *(Sitting)* O K. *(Noticing error messages)* "The window password you typed is incorrect." That's why! It has a blue color on the white stripe. Look at it. I hate it.

TARA: *(From her room)* It's highlighted. Just write it again.

(The computer beeps.)

STANLEY: Now it's ringing.

TARA: *(From her room)* Click on it.

(STANLEY *clicks. The computer beeps.*)

STANLEY: It keeps ringing the bell.

(The computer boots up with a symphonic sound.)

STANLEY: Oh, it's singing, now we're finished. OH! Here we are! I got the screen!

TARA: *(From her room)* You did it!

STANLEY: I don't know how I did it. It just came on accidentally.

(TARA *enters with more luggage.*)

TARA: Yay!

STANLEY: Don't start that.

TARA: What?

STANLEY: Too much use of the word "Yay".

TARA: By me?

STANLEY: In general. In the whole fuckin' world. *(About screen)* Now it says virus.

TARA: It's just checking everything.

STANLEY: *(Reading from the screen)* "HP 2.0 Screen Set Up." It's giving me a lecture now. I wanna erase that.

TARA: Try to shut it down now.

STANLEY: If I unplug it, it won't shut down?

TARA: That'll damage it.

STANLEY: The only thing I learned was how to play gently with that arrow. *(Demonstrating with his index finger in the air)* I go in circles. The arrow goes in circles. Don't google me right away, O K? I don't wanna miss your messages.

TARA: I'm gonna email you first thing, and let you know I got there O K.

STANLEY: What you're gonna do is call me. When you get there, and then every Sunday.

TARA: I have to give you an incentive to check your email, Dad, or you'll get lazy. *(She puts on a partially zipped jacket by stepping into it feet first.)*

STANLEY: Is the zipper broken?

TARA: The zipper at the bottom isn't doing very well. I don't wanna get stuck.

STANLEY: You got everything?

TARA: Yeah.

STANLEY: You don't sound too excited.

TARA: I'm a little nervous.

STANLEY: Nothin' to be nervous about.

TARA: What did they do to the street outside?

STANLEY: They dug it up.

TARA: Did a water main break or something?

STANLEY: No. They're puttin' in a new street.

TARA: They really scraped it.

STANLEY: They scrape it so the new stuff grabs. Can't just pour it on top, or it won't bond. Then Berks Products brings that cement mixed with gravel, spreads it hot, pouring out of a truck. It don't come out smooth neither, they gotta rake it, and rake it, it's sticky as all hell, tar and gravel, stinks from here to Kunzler Township. But that goes away after a while, and you got your fresh street, two streamers of paint smack dab in the middle. It's somethin', lookin' at it, right when it's done, you know, when it has that sparkle to it. It's like nothin' can mess with it. You know? It's gonna be right there, underneath everything, it's gonna stay right there, no matter what, forever.

END OF PLAY

CPSIA information can be obtained
at www.ICGtesting.com
Printed in the USA
LVOW10s2143150617

538315LV00010B/458/P